One Blue Hen
Colour Rhymes

Chosen by Kate Ruttle and Richard Brown
Illustrated by Niki Hayward

CAMBRIDGE
UNIVERSITY PRESS

Little Blue Ben

Little Blue Ben lives in a den.

He has one blue cat and one blue hen.

The hen lays blue eggs, nine or ten.

Where can I find Little Blue Ben?

Five Pretty Rose Trees

Five pretty rose trees
in my garden bed.

Three of them are snowy white.
Two of them are red.

Silver and Gold

Red stockings, blue stockings,

shoes tied up with silver.

A golden crown upon my head

and a gold ring on my finger.

Little Nut Tree

I had a little nut tree,
nothing would it bear

but a silver nutmeg
and a golden pear.

The King of Spain's daughter
came to visit me,

and all for the sake
of my little nut tree.